The publishers are grateful for permission to reproduce the following material:

Reprinted with the permission of Margaret K. McElderry Books, an imprint of Simon & Schuster Children's Publishing Division, from *We're Going on a Bear Hunt* by Michael Rosen, illustrated by Helen Oxenbury. Text copyright © 1989 Michael Rosen. Illustrations copyright © 1989 Helen Oxenbury.

From *This Is the Bear and the Picnic Lunch* by Sarah Hayes. Text copyright © 1988 by Sarah Hayes. Illustrations copyright © 1988 by Helen Craig. By permission of Little, Brown and Company.

First edition 1995

Library of Congress Cataloging-in-Publication Data is available.

ISBN 1-56402-653-1

4 6 8 10 9 7 5 3

Printed in Mexico

Candlewick Press
2067 Massachusetts Avenue
Cambridge, Massachusetts 02140

THE CANDLEWICK
BOOK OF
BEAR
STORIES

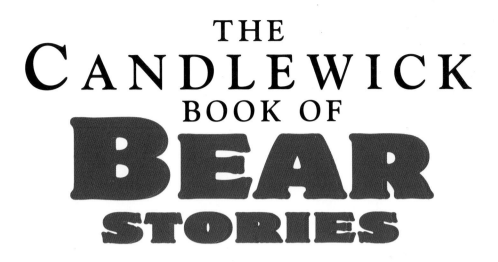

CANDLEWICK PRESS
CAMBRIDGE, MASSACHUSETTS

CONTENTS

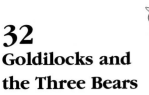

We're Going on

retold by Michael Rosen

We're going on a bear hunt.
We're going to catch a big one.
What a beautiful day!
We're not scared.

  Oh-oh! Grass!
Long, wavy grass.
We can't go over it.
We can't go under it.

Oh, no!

We've got to
  go through it!

Swishy swashy!
  Swishy swashy!
Swishy swashy!

We're going on a bear hunt.
We're going to catch a big one.
What a beautiful day!
We're not scared.

  Oh-oh! A river!
A deep, cold river.
We can't go over it.
We can't go under it.

Oh, no!

We've got to
  go through it!

Splash splosh!
  Splash splosh!
Splash splosh!

We're going on a bear hunt.
We're going to catch a big one.
What a beautiful day!
We're not scared.

  Oh-oh! Mud!
Thick, oozy mud.
We can't go over it.
We can't go under it.

Oh, no!

We've got to
  go through it!

Squelch squerch!
  Squelch squerch!
Squelch squerch!

a Bear Hunt

illustrated by Helen Oxenbury

We're going on a bear hunt.
We're going to catch a big one.
What a beautiful day!
We're not scared.

   Oh-oh! A forest!
A big, dark forest.
We can't go over it.
We can't go under it.

Oh, no!

We've got to
   go through it!

Stumble trip!
   Stumble trip!
   Stumble trip!

We're going on a bear hunt.
We're going to catch a big one.
What a beautiful day!
We're not scared.

   Oh-oh! A snowstorm!
A swirling, whirling snowstorm.
We can't go over it.
We can't go under it.

Oh, no!

We've got to
   go through it!

Hoooo woooo!
   Hoooo woooo!
Hoooo woooo!

We're going on a bear hunt.
We're going to catch a big one.
What a beautiful day!
We're not scared.

   Oh-oh! A cave!
A narrow, gloomy cave.
We can't go over it.
We can't go under it.

Oh, no!

We've got to
   go through it!

Tiptoe!
   Tiptoe!
Tiptoe!

WHAT'S THAT?

One shiny wet nose!
Two big furry ears!
Two big goggly eyes!

IT'S A BEAR!!!!

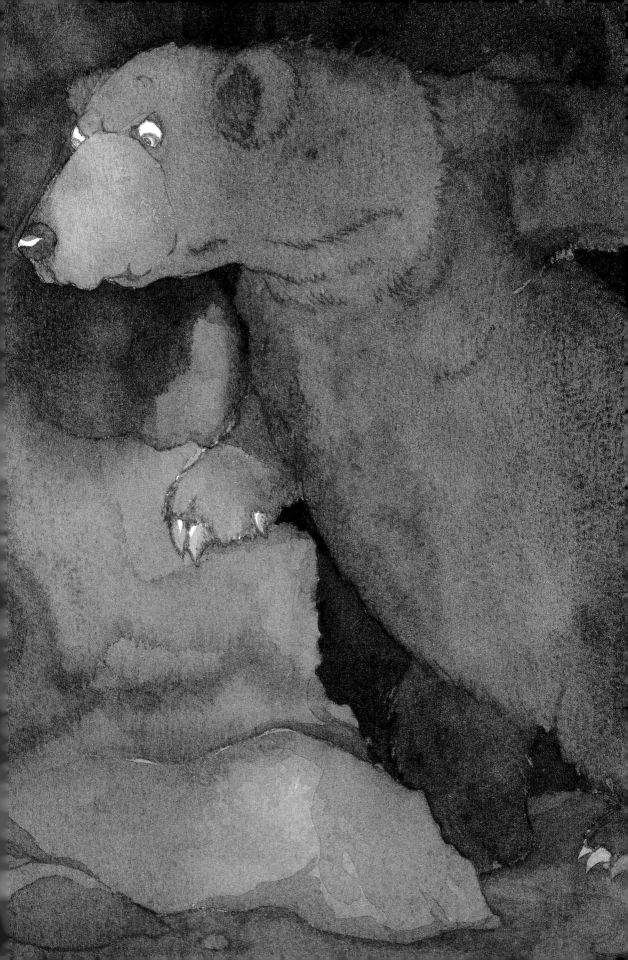

 Quick!
Back through
the cave!
Tiptoe! Tiptoe!

 Back through
the snowstorm!
Hoooo wooooo!
Hoooo wooooo!

 Back through
the forest!
Stumble trip!
Stumble trip!

 Back through
the mud!
Squelch squerch!
Squelch squerch!

 Back through
the river!
Splash splosh!
Splash splosh!

 Back through
the grass!
Swishy swashy!
Swishy swashy!

Get to our front door.
Open the door. Up the stairs.

Oh, no! We forgot to
shut the door. Back downstairs.

Shut the door. Back upstairs.
Into the bedroom.

Into bed.
Under the covers.

13

We're not going on

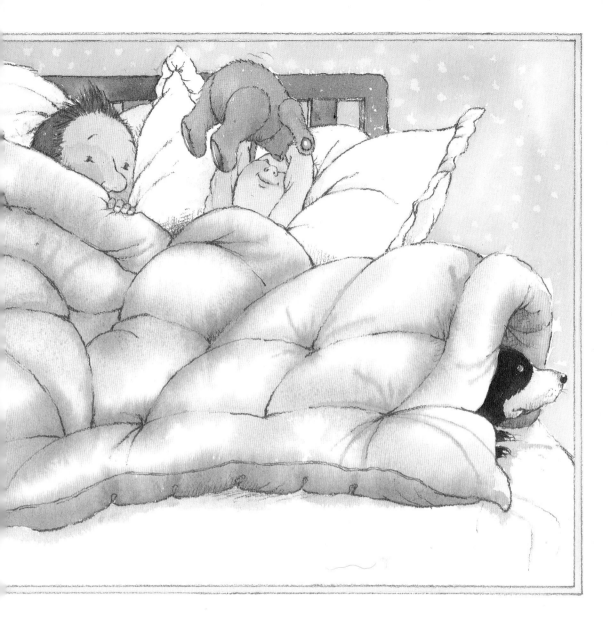

a bear hunt again.

THIS IS THE BEAR AND THE PICNIC LUNCH

Sarah Hayes illustrated by Helen Craig

This is the dog who
sneaked past the chair
toward the picnic lunch
and the brave guard bear.

This is the boy
who packed a lunch
of sandwiches, chips
and an apple to crunch.

This is the bear
with his eyes half closed
who did not notice
the dog's black nose.

This is the bear
who guarded the box
while the boy went to find
his shoes and his socks.

I'm a guard bear!

onto the table . . .
down to the floor . . .
and off to hide
behind the door . . .

This is the bear
who was sound asleep
when the dog took off with
a tremendous leap . . .

and all that he left
of the picnic lunch
was an empty box and
an apple to crunch.

GERONIMO!

This is the boy
who looked everywhere
for his lunch and his dog
and his brave guard bear.

This is the boy
who tried to be angry

This is the boy
who heard the munch
of a dog and a bear
eating a lunch.

but decided instead
he was terribly hungry.

18

This is the boy who packed a new lunch
of sandwiches, chips and an apple to crunch.
And this is the bear who said, "Haven't you guessed?
Picnics indoors are really the best!"

19

swing

drop

skip

bounce

push

pull

dive

slump

21

LASKA THE POLAR BEAR

Derek Hall • illustrated by John Butler

Laska the polar bear is big enough to leave the den where he was born. For the first time he plays outside in the soft snow.

Soon it is time to go to the sea for food. Laska's mother is hungry. He rides high on her back, gripping her fur with excitement.

While his mother is busy eating, Laska wanders off. He stands up on his hind legs, as tall as he can, to look out over the Arctic Ocean.

Suddenly the ice breaks! A small ice floe carries Laska away from the land, and he is too young to swim! He whimpers for his mother.

She roars to her cub in alarm. Bravely he leaps across the gap toward her. It is almost too far! His paws slither on the icy shore.

Just in time his mother grasps him by the neck. She hauls him, dripping wet, from the water. Laska hangs limp and miserable from her strong jaws.

On firm land again, he shakes himself like a dog to dry his fur. His mother wants to find a safe place to sleep. Laska follows her like a shadow.

Now Laska is hungry. His mother feeds him with her milk. Then he snuggles up to her warm body and goes to sleep.

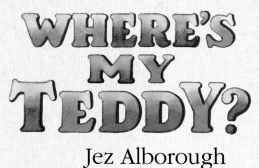

WHERE'S MY TEDDY?

Jez Alborough

Eddie's off to
find his teddy.
Eddie's teddy's
name is Freddie.

He lost him in the
woods somewhere.
It's dark and
horrible in there.

"Help!" said Eddie.
"I'm scared already!
I want my bed!
I want my teddy!"

He tiptoed
on and on until . . .
something made
him stop quite still.

Look out! he thought.
There's something there!

WHAT'S THAT?

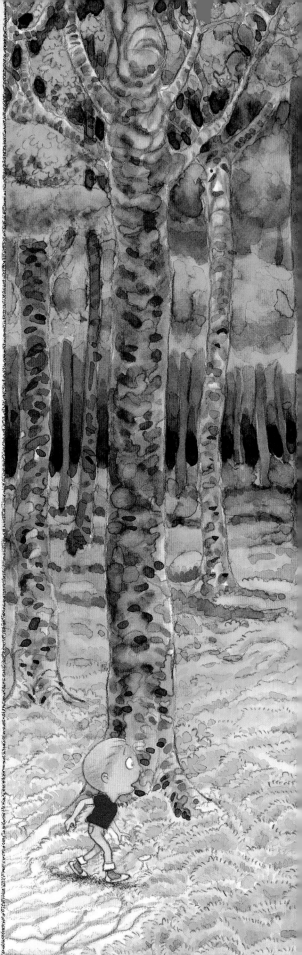

A GIANT TEDDY BEAR!

"Is it Freddie?" said Eddie.
"What a surprise!
How *did* you get to
be this size?"

"You're too big to huddle
and cuddle," he said,
"and I'll never fit both
of us into my bed."

Then out of the darkness,
clearer and clearer,
the sound of sobbing
came nearer and nearer.

Soon the whole woods
could hear the voice bawl,
"How did you get to be
tiny and small?

You're too small to
huddle and cuddle," it said,
"and you'll only get lost
in my giant-sized bed!"

It was a gigantic bear
and a tiny teddy
stomping toward the
giant teddy and Eddie.

"MY TED!"
gasped the bear.

"A BEAR!"
screamed Eddie.

"A BOY!"
yelled the bear.

"MY TEDDY!"
cried Eddie.

Then they ran and they ran
through the dark woods
back to their homes
as fast as they could . . .

all the way back
to their snuggly beds,
where they huddled
and cuddled their
own little teds.

31

Goldilocks
and the
Three Bears

Charlotte Voake

Once upon a time there were three bears—Daddy Bear, Mommy Bear, and little Baby Bear. They all lived together in a cottage in the woods. Every morning the three bears had porridge for breakfast. They each had their own bowl—a great big bowl for Daddy Bear, a medium-

sized bowl for Mommy Bear, and a little baby bowl for little Baby Bear. One morning they sat down to eat their porridge and found that it was too hot.

"Let's go for a walk in the woods," said Mommy Bear. "When we get back, our porridge will be cool enough to eat."

No sooner had the three bears gone out than a little girl with golden hair came up to the cottage. Her name was Goldilocks. She pushed open the door and walked straight in.

"Oh! Lovely porridge! My favorite!" she said. First Goldilocks tasted the porridge in the great big bowl. "Much too hot!" she said. Next she tasted the porridge in

the medium-sized bowl. "Much too salty!" she said. Last she tasted the porridge in the little baby bowl. "Just exactly right!" she said, and ate it all up, every bit.

"Now," said Goldilocks, looking around the room, "I will try one of these chairs."

First she sat on the great big chair. "Much too hard!" she said. Next she sat on the medium-sized chair. "Much too soft!" she said. Last she sat on the little baby chair. "Just exactly right!" she said. But then *crack! splinter! crash!*—the chair broke all to pieces.

"Now," said Goldilocks, "I will go and lie down, because I do feel very tired." She went upstairs to the three bears' bedroom.

"Oh! Oh! Oh!" she said. "Three lovely beds to choose from!" First she tried the great big bed. "Much too high!" she said. Next she tried the medium-sized bed. "Much too lumpy!" she said. Last she tried the little baby bed. "Just exactly right!" she said, and she got right in and pulled up the covers, and soon she was fast asleep.

Before long the three bears came back from their walk. They were all very hungry. Daddy Bear looked at his great big bowl.

"Someone's been eating my porridge!" he said in a great big voice. Mommy Bear looked at her medium-sized bowl.

"Someone's been eating my porridge!" she said in a medium-sized voice.

Then little Baby Bear looked at his little baby bowl and said, "Someone's been eating my porridge and has EATEN IT ALL UP!"

"Look at this!" Daddy Bear said in a great big voice. "Someone's been sitting on my chair!"

"Someone's been sitting on my chair, too," said Mommy Bear in a medium-sized voice.

"And someone's been sitting on my chair," said little Baby Bear in a little baby voice, "and they've BROKEN IT ALL TO BITS!"

The three bears ran upstairs.

"Someone's been lying on my bed," Daddy Bear said in a great big voice.

"Someone's been lying on my bed, too," Mommy Bear said in a medium-sized voice.

"And someone's been lying on my bed," said little Baby Bear in a little baby voice, "and SHE'S STILL HERE!"

Goldilocks woke up and saw the three bears all looking down at her. So she leapt out of bed, ran across the room, and jumped straight out of the window. Then she ran home as fast as she possibly could.

And the three bears never saw her again.

Midnight Teddies

Dana Kubick

Teddy had been Jessica's special bear for as long as he could remember. Wherever Jessica went, Teddy went too—and Jessica's favorite place was the attic.

Today, Jessica had the key to the big old trunk, which she had never opened. In it she found hats as big as frying pans and silky gowns that had come all the way from China. Jessica always dressed up Teddy. He liked that!

What Teddy didn't like was to be left alone in the attic. In fact, it had never ever happened before. But this evening, when it was time for bed, Jessica simply forgot Teddy. And although he was an extremely clever bear, Teddy could not move a single muscle until midnight, the hour when toys can come to life. To make matters worse, a book was poking him in the back.

Even more annoying, Teddy distinctly heard the trunk say, "Help!"

It seemed a long time before the downstairs clock struck twelve. Then Teddy felt himself shiver and quiver. He managed to move the uncomfortable book just a little.

"Help!" cried the voice again.

Teddy had never heard of a talking trunk, and his fur stood on end. Then he realized there was someone inside it!

"Who's there?" he whispered, peering over the edge.

To Teddy's surprise, out climbed two strange, dusty bears.

"I'm Theodore," said the one in the sailor suit.

"I'm Ned," said the one in the old-fashioned cardigan. Ned was coming

unstitched in several places.

"We're so glad to see you. We were put away years and years ago, when our children grew up. It's been terribly boring closed in the trunk with no one to play with."

"When Theodore can't think of anything else to do, he tickles," complained Ned.

"Well," said Teddy. "Tonight we can play together."

Because he was the bear of the house, Teddy led the way. They all went down the stairs—bumpety-bump, bumpety-bump—one step after another, and landed in a heap at the bottom. Clouds of dust flew up around the two old bears, especially Theodore, who sneezed. *"Achoo! Achoo!"*

Teddy was alarmed. What if someone had heard the thumps and bumps and sneezes? He tiptoed to Jessica's bedroom and opened the door. Silly Lily, the cat, opened one eye, but otherwise no one stirred. He opened the next door.

"Who's that?" asked Ned.

"Jessica's brother," said Teddy. "But he doesn't like bears. He likes jets and rockets."

"What's a jet?" said Theodore.

"What's a rocket?" said Ned.

Teddy stared at them. What a long time they had been in the trunk if they didn't know about jets and rockets!

The two old bears were even more puzzled when Teddy suggested they play in the bathroom. Theodore tried all the strange, shiny handles.

Suddenly, water showered down from above his head! Poor Ned was soaked. He had wanted to play with the plastic ducks and fish and boats— plastic was something very different indeed!

38

Downstairs, in the kitchen, there were even more knobs and switches and handles. Teddy opened the refrigerator and a light came on.

"It's magic!" said Theodore.

"No," said Teddy. "It's electricity."

Theodore shut the refrigerator door, then opened it, shut it, and opened it, just to see the light go off and on. He couldn't reach the magic light, so he stood on his tallest tiptoes, grabbed the shelf, and pulled himself up.

Whoosh! Down came the tub of yogurt. *Zoom!* went Teddy . . . and caught it just in time.

Yogurt was Teddy's favorite and he took a little taste (or two, or three) before he put the tub back. He didn't notice Theodore clinging to the refrigerator door. And certainly no one saw the jar of strawberry jam—until it was suddenly all over the floor!

Teddy was horrified. "Quickly!" he gasped. "Get a cloth! Get a mop!"

The three bears wiped and mopped until there wasn't a bit of strawberry jam left on the floor. By then, Teddy had decided that the kitchen was a rather frightening place.

The next day, as soon as it was light, Jessica realized that Teddy was missing and she ran to the attic.

But the living room wasn't any safer. Without warning, Theodore turned on the television and filled the room with noise.

"Turn it off!" Teddy shouted.

But poor Theodore and Ned simply stared at the television in amazement.

Teddy flicked off the switch himself, but not quickly enough. They heard footsteps in the hall. The door opened and someone big peered in and then went away again.

"Let's go back upstairs," Teddy said, and the others agreed.

"Poor Teddy!" she said. "I forgot you." Of course Teddy couldn't say a word.

Then Jessica noticed some fur peeking from under her dress-up clothes. "Who are you?" she asked, pulling out the two old bears.

And then she discovered something else—an album of photographs in the lining of the trunk. She saw pictures of Theodore, all clean and new, and there was Ned on a picnic.

"You're family bears!" Jessica said, and she took all three to her room.

There, Jessica brushed and sponged the old bears. She put a button on Theodore's trousers and gave Ned new stitches where he was coming undone. She put up their photographs and added one of herself with Teddy.

She sat the bears together on her bed. Already they looked like best friends.

And so they were. The only thing that puzzled Jessica was that all three bears smelled faintly of strawberry jam.

LITTLE MO

MARTIN WADDELL
illustrated by
JILL BARTON

Little Mo looked at the ice and she liked it.

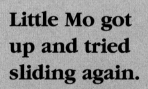

Little Mo got up and tried sliding again.

BUMP!

BUMP!

A Big One came to help her.

More Big Ones came out onto the ice, sliding and gliding around Little Mo.

They were her friends, all of them. It was nice on the ice and she loved it.

The Big Ones whizzed and they whirled and they twisted and

twirled and they raced and they jumped.

BUMP!

BUMP!

Little Mo started to cry and she turned away. She didn't like the ice anymore.

"It was all *my* idea," Little Mo said to herself.

The Big Ones got tired
and went home.
They forgot Little Mo.

Little Mo looked
at the ice and
she liked it again.
She slid and . . . and . . .
she fell.

BUMP!

She got up and then
she did it again without
falling, and again and
again and again . . .
all by herself, sliding
around on the ice . . .

and Little Mo loved it.

A VISIT FROM BEAR

Colin Threadgall

One hot day, Panda and Takin were dozing peacefully in the forest. Bear peeked through the bamboo. He had come to pay a visit.

Bear sneaked up behind Panda. **"Wakey! Wakey!"**
"Put me down, Bear!" said Panda.

Takin woke up too. "Oh dear," he sighed. "Bear always means trouble."
"Let's dance, Takin," said Bear.
"Put me down, Bear!" said Takin.

"Hello!" boomed Bear into a hole in a tree. "Anybody home?"
"Yes," said Marten crossly.
"Go away, Bear!"
Bear climbed the tree.
"Oh, stop that, Bear!" said Tufted Deer.
Then Bear shook a branch. "Shake-a-leg, Squirrels, shake-a-leg!"

"I'll dig you a hole," Bear said to Hog Badger.
"No thank you, Bear," said Hog Badger. But Bear wasn't listening, and he dug a hole anyway.

Bear lumbered around, chasing the pheasants. There was no peace and quiet in the forest anymore.

49

"Something must be done about Bear," said Panda. "Come on, Takin. I have an idea."
He walked into a clearing and picked up some sticks. "What are you doing, Panda?" asked Bear.

"Trying to throw sticks over that tall rock," said Panda.
"Silly Panda! You're not strong enough for that," said Bear, snatching a stick from Panda's paw. "I'll show you how a bear can throw sticks, just watch me."

But Panda and Takin didn't stay to watch. "RUN, Takin!" said Panda. Bear threw the sticks hard and high, one after the other. He looked around—where were Panda and Takin?

Bear turned back to the rock . . . and stared.
A row of furious monkeys stared back at him.
They had been sunbathing on the other side of
the rock and the sticks had landed on their heads.
"See how *you* like sticks on your head, Bear!"
they screeched. Poor Bear fled. The monkeys chased
Bear out of the forest and down the hill.

The animals sighed with relief. There
would be peace and quiet in the forest
again—until Bear paid them another visit!

51

Sailor Bear

Martin Waddell   illustrated by Virginia Austin

Small Bear was a bear in a sailor suit who was lost and had no one to play with. "Now what shall I do?" wondered Small Bear.

He thought and he thought. Then he looked at his suit, and he *knew* what to do.

"I'll be a sailor and sail on the sea!" decided Small Bear. But he didn't have a boat. "Now what shall I do?" wondered Small Bear.

He thought and he thought. Then he looked at the sea, and he *knew* what to do.

"I'll go and get one!" decided Small Bear. He went to the harbor, but the boats there were too big for a bear. "Now what shall I do?" wondered Small Bear. He thought and he thought. Then he looked around the shore, and he *knew* what to do.

"Small bears need small boats, so I'll make one!" decided Small Bear. He made a boat from some pieces of wood and half a barrel. He called it

"Bear's Boat," and he took it down to the sea. BUT . . .
the sea looked too big for his boat. "Now what shall
I do?" wondered Small Bear.
He thought and he thought. Then he looked at a
puddle, and he *knew* what to do.

"Small boats need small seas, so I'll find one!"
decided Small Bear. He went to the park, where
he found a small sea, AND . . .

Small Bear sailed in "Bear's Boat" by the light of
the moon. BUT . . .

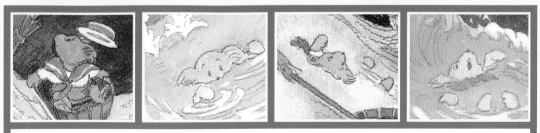

the sea grew too rough! "Bear's Boat" rocked and it rolled and it shattered and SANK!

So he swam and swam until he reached the shore, where he lay on a rock all shivering and cold. "Now what shall I do?" wondered Small Bear.
He thought and he thought. Then he sighed at the moon, for he didn't know what to do!

"I'm sick of the sea, so I think I'll give up!" decided Small Bear with a sniff.
He curled up by the rock and went sadly to sleep all alone.

The very next morning a little girl came and found Small Bear, and she hugged him and took him home and set him to dry by the fire.

"Now what shall I do?" wondered Small Bear.

He thought and he thought. Then he looked around the home, and he *knew* what to do.

"I'm FOUND, and I have someone to play with, so I'll stay where I am!" decided Small Bear, and he cuddled up close to the girl and he stayed . . .

and he never went back to the sea!

wobble

drip

scrub

slop

wipe

wobble

pop

POP

John Burningham

bump

swat

squeeze

splash

bubble

stumble

First Snow

KIM LEWIS

"Wake up, Sara," whispered Mommy. "Daddy's not very well today. I'm going to feed the sheep on the hill. Would you and Teddy like to come?"

Outside, the dogs were ready and waiting, bright-eyed and eager to go. Frost nipped the air. It was early winter and the rooks were calling. A wind was starting to blow. Through the gate and up the steep path, Mommy and Sara climbed.

The sky turned grayer and the air grew colder. The dogs raced on ahead. As they climbed higher, Sara looked back. The farmhouse seemed very small.

At the top of the hill stood the lone pine tree, bent by years of winter winds. Mommy and Sara stopped below it to rest. The air went suddenly still.

"We're on top of the world," said Mommy, hugging Sara. "Just you and me and Teddy."

Across the valley the sky turned white. Snowflakes lightly danced in the air.

"Look, look!" Sara laughed. She watched as a snowflake fell on her mitten.

"We'd better feed the sheep," said Mommy, "before it snows too hard." Sara helped Mommy spread hay on the ground. The sheep were hungry and pushed all around them. Sara tried catching the snow in her hands, but the wind swirled the snowflakes in front of her eyes. Then the snow fell faster and stung Sara's cheeks. The air grew thick and white.

"Come on," said Mommy, her hand out to Sara. "The sheep are

all right and we must go home before the snow gets too deep."

The dogs disappeared through the flying snow. Snow blotted out the lone pine. Mommy and Sara started down the path, hugging close to the wall. Then suddenly Sara stopped.

"Oh no, where's Teddy?" she cried.

Mommy looked back. Behind them the snow was filling their tracks.

"We can't look for Teddy now," said Mommy. She whistled for the dogs and started to walk, but Sara sat still in the snow.

Sara, hugging him tight. Mommy picked up Sara and Teddy.

"Now we can all go home," she said.

As they came down the hill, the air cleared of snow. The sky began turning blue. Sara and Mommy could see the farmhouse again, standing snug in the yard. The world all around them was white and still.

Then out of the whiteness, one of the dogs appeared. She was gently carrying Teddy.

"Oh, Teddy," cried

Sara and Mommy
warmed up by the fire.
Then they took Daddy
his breakfast in bed.
"Who's fed the sheep?"

Daddy asked them.
Sara snuggled up
beside him.
"Mommy and Teddy
and me!" she said.

Hello, Good-bye

David Lloyd   illustrated by Louise Voce

A tree stood quietly in the sunshine.
A big brown bear stepped up.
"Hello!" he said, very loudly.
Two bees flew over.
"Hello! Hello!" they said,
very busily.

Hello!

hello!   hello!

Along came a big red bird.
What did the bird say?
"Hello!"—very
quickly.

Hello!

HELLO

Hello...

hello...

hello!

hello

Soon voices all over the tree
were saying, "Hello!"
Little voices on the leaves
said, "Hello!"
Squeaky voices on the branches
said, "Hello!"
Deep-down voices among the
roots said, "Hello!"

hello!

HELLO

hello

hello

Suddenly a drop of rain fell on the bear's nose. Splash! Raindrops fell all over the bear. Splash! Splash! Splash!

"Good-bye! Good-bye!" said the two bees, very busily.

"Good-bye!" said the big red bird, very quickly.

Good-bye!

Good-bye!

What did all the voices
on the tree say?
What did the bear say,
very loudly?
"Good-bye!"

Good-bye!

Everyone
had gone.
The tree stood
quietly again.
"Hello, rain!"
it said, very, very
quietly.

Good-bye!

EAT YOUR DINNER!

Virginia Miller

George came looking for Bartholomew with his dinner.

"Dinner's ready, Ba," he said. "Have you washed your face and hands?"

"Nah!" said Bartholomew.

George said, "Sit up, Ba, and eat your dinner."

"Nah, nah, nah, nah, NAH!" said Bartholomew.

Eat your dinner

George said in a big voice.

Bartholomew ate one spoonful, then he had a little rest.

George sat down at the table and began to eat his dinner.

Bartholomew watched until George had finished.

Then George left the table and returned with a large honey cake.

He cut a slice and ate it. When he had finished, he took the rest away.

Suddenly Bartholomew thought, *Eat your dinner!*

He thought of the honey cake with the pretty pink icing and the cherry on top . . . and he licked his bowl perfectly clean.

He went to find George.

"You've finished, Ba!" George said.

"Nah!" said Bartholomew. George smiled and gave him the slice of cake with the cherry on top.

When the Teddy Bears Came

Martin Waddell • illustrated by **Penny Dale**

When the new baby came to Tom's house, the teddy bears started coming. Alice Bear came in the crib. Tom kissed Alice Bear and the baby.

Ozzie Bear came with Uncle Jack. Ozzie Bear had a flag and a hat.

Ozzie Bear sat on a chair, where he could take care of the baby.

Then Miss Wilkins came with Sam Bear in his sailor suit. Sam Bear sat on the chair beside Ozzie Bear.

"*I* want to give our baby a bear!" Tom said. So he gave the new baby his Huggy. Tom told Mom, "Huggy can take care of our baby now." Tom put Huggy beside Alice Bear.

Rockwell and Dudley Bear came in a van. They were a little squashed. Tom unsquashed them for the new baby. Rockwell and  Dudley Bear went on the chair beside Ozzie Bear and Sam Bear.

Gran brought Bodger Bear from her attic.
"That's my Bodger Bear!" Dad said.

Mom said, "Look at our baby with all of these bears!"

Tom looked at the bears. Alice Bear, Ozzie Bear, Sam Bear and Huggy, Rockwell and Dudley Bear, and Dad's Bodger Bear, all on the couch beside Mom and the baby.

"There's no room for *me*," Tom said to Mom.

Mom smiled and said, "Come here, Tom, and sit on
my knee. You and I can take care of the bears.
It's Dad's turn to take care of the baby."

And that's what they did. When the new baby came to Tom's house, they all took turns taking care of the bears . . .

and the baby.

Ben and the Bear

Chris Riddell

One day Ben was bored.
He put on a big winter coat.
He put on a floppy hat.
Then he set off
into the snow.

After a while he met a
bear. The bear said, "What
a lovely coat." Ben said,
"Come home for tea."

Some of the way the
bear carried Ben.

Some of the way
Ben tried to carry
the bear.

The bear took Ben's coat. Ben and the bear sat down at the table. The bear poured the tea. Ben passed the sugar cubes. The bear ate them all up. They ate some bread. And then they ate some honey.

The bear said, "Let's dance."
So they did.

Ben said, "What a mess!"
The bear said, "Let's
clean up."

They washed
the dishes.
They put the
dishes away.
They folded
the tablecloth.

Ben said,
"That looks neat."
The bear said, "What
should we do with the coat?"
Ben said, "You can have the coat."
The bear said, "Tomorrow
you must come to
tea at my house."

My Old Teddy

Dom Mansell

My old Teddy's leg came off.
Poor old Teddy!

I took him to the
Teddy doctor.
She made
Teddy better.

My old Teddy's
arm came off.
*Poor old
Teddy!*

I took him to the
Teddy doctor.
She made
Teddy better.

My old Teddy's ear came off.
Poor old Teddy!

I took him to the
Teddy doctor.
She made
Teddy better.

 Then poor old Teddy's
head came off.

The Teddy doctor said
"Teddy's had enough now.
Teddy has to rest."

 The Teddy
doctor
gave me
a new
Teddy.

I love my new Teddy very much,
but I love poor old Teddy best.

Dear old,
poor old
Teddy.

Let's Go Home, Little Bear

Martin Waddell • illustrated by Barbara Firth

Once there were two bears. Big Bear and Little Bear. Big Bear is the big bear and Little Bear is the little bear. They went for a walk in the woods.

They walked and they walked and they walked until Big Bear said, "Let's go home, Little Bear." So they started back home on the path through the woods.

PLOD PLOD PLOD went Big Bear, plodding along. Little Bear ran on in front, jumping and sliding and having great fun.

And then . . . Little Bear stopped and he listened and then he turned around and he looked.

"Come on, Little Bear," said Big Bear, but Little Bear didn't stir.

"I thought I heard something!" Little Bear said.

"What did you hear?" said Big Bear.

"Plod, plod, plod," said Little Bear. "I think it's a Plodder!"

Big Bear turned around and he listened and looked. No Plodder was there.

"Let's go home, Little Bear," said Big Bear. "The plod was my feet in the snow."

They set off again on the path through the woods.

PLOD PLOD PLOD went Big Bear with Little Bear walking beside him, just

glancing a bit, now and again.

And then . . . Little Bear stopped and he listened and then he turned around and he looked.

"Come on, Little Bear," said Big Bear, but Little Bear didn't stir.

"I thought I heard something!" Little Bear said.

"What did you hear?" said Big Bear.

"Drip, drip, drip," said Little Bear. "I think it's a Dripper!"

Big Bear turned around and he listened and looked. No Dripper was there.

"Let's go home, Little Bear," said Big Bear. "That was the ice as it dripped in the stream."

They set off again on the path through the woods.

PLOD PLOD PLOD went Big Bear with Little Bear closer beside him.

And then . . . Little Bear stopped and he listened

and then he turned around and he looked.

"Come on, Little Bear," said Big Bear, but Little Bear didn't stir.

"I know I heard something this time!" Little Bear said.

"What did you hear?" said Big Bear.

"Plop, plop, plop," said Little Bear. "I think it's a Plopper."

Big Bear turned around and he listened and looked. No Plopper was there.

"Let's go home, Little Bear," said Big Bear. "That was the snow plopping down from a branch."

PLOD PLOD PLOD went Big Bear along the path through the woods.

But Little Bear walked slower and slower and at last he sat down in the snow.

"Come on, Little Bear," said Big Bear. "It is time we were both back home."

But Little Bear sat and said nothing.

"Come on and be carried," said Big Bear.

Big Bear put Little Bear high up on his back and set off down the path through the woods.

WOO WOO WOO

"It is only the wind, Little Bear," said Big Bear and he walked on down the path.

CREAK CREAK CREAK

"It is only the trees, Little Bear," said Big Bear and he walked on down the path.

PLOD PLOD PLOD

"It is only the sound of my feet again," said Big Bear, and he plodded on and on and on until they came back home to their cave.

Big Bear and Little Bear went down into the dark,

the dark of their own Bear Cave.

"Just stay there, Little Bear," said Big Bear, putting Little Bear in the Bear Chair with a blanket to keep him warm. Big Bear stirred up the fire from the embers and lighted the lamps and made the Bear Cave all cozy again.

"Now tell me a story," Little Bear said.

And Big Bear sat down in the Bear Chair with Little Bear curled up on his lap. And he told a story of Plodders and Drippers and Ploppers and the sounds of the snow in the woods, and this Little Bear and this Big Bear plodding all the way . . . HOME!